PREFACE

This report sets forth the statutes, regulations, and Executive Branch directives that define and govern access to Sensitive But Unclassified (SBU) information. Although there is growing concern in the post 9/11 world that guidelines for the protection of SBU (often referred to as Sensitive Homeland Security Information) are needed, a uniform legal definition or set of procedures applicable to all Federal government agencies does not now exist. Regulations are reported to be under development in the Office of Management and Budget and the Department of Homeland Security.

The dissemination of SBU technology is regulated through export controls administered by the Departments of Commerce and State. This report outlines the general applicability of these controls, as well as their applicability to missile and nuclear technology. This report also delineates regulations and directives applicable to the Department of Defense, Department of Energy, Federal Aviation Administration (and Transportation Security Administration), Nuclear Regulatory Commission, and Department of State.

TABLE OF CONTENTS

PREFACE i

EXECUTIVE BRANCH DIRECTIVES REGARDING CLASSIFICATION AND
PROTECTION OF FEDERAL INFORMATION 1
    Executive Orders 1
    White House Memoranda 1
    Presidential and National Security Directives 2
        Presidential Directive/NSC 24 2
        *National Security Decision Directive 189 – National Policy on the Transfer of
        Scientific, Technical and Engineering Information* 2
        *National Telecommunications and Information Systems Security Policy (NTISSP)
        No.2 – National Policy on Protection of Sensitive, but Unclassified Information in
        Federal Government Telecommunications and Automated Information Systems* 3
        *National Security Decision Directive 145 – National Policy on Telecommunications
        and Automated Information Systems Security* 3
        *National Security Directive 42 – National Policy for the Security of National
        Security Telecommunications and Information Systems* 4
    Future Initiatives 4

FEDERAL LAWS APPLICABLE TO ALL GOVERNMENT AGENCIES REGARDING
SENSITIVE BUT UNCLASSIFIED INFORMATION 5
    Freedom of Information Act of 1966, as Amended (5 USC 552) 5
        Attorney General FOIA Memorandum 5
        Exemptions to FOIA 5
    Federal Information Security Management Act of 2002 (FISMA)(Public Law 107-347,
    Title III, 116 Stat. 2899, 2946) 6
    Homeland Security Act of 2002 (Public Law 107-296, 116 Stat. 2135) 8

EXPORT CONTROLS 10
    Arms Export Control Act/International Traffic in Arms Regulations (ITAR) 10
    Export Administration Act/Export Administration Regulations (EAR) 12

NUCLEAR NONPROLIFERATION 12
    Nuclear Nonproliferation Act (P.L. 95-242) 12
    Nuclear Proliferation Prevention Act (P.L. 103-236, Title VIII) 13
    Iran Nonproliferation Act of 2000 (P.L. 106-278) 13

MISSILE TECHNOLOGY 13
    Missile Technology Control Regime 13
    National Defense Authorization Act for FY 1991 (P.L. 101-510,Title XVII – Missile
    Technology Controls) 14
    National Defense Authorization Act for FY 1999 (P.L. 105-261, Title XV, Subtitle
    B – Satellite Export Controls) 14

DEPARTMENT OF DEFENSE 15
    Unclassifed Information – General 15
    Technical Data 17
    Unclassified Controlled Nuclear Information 19

DEPARTMENT OF ENERGY 20

FEDERAL AVIATION ADMINISTRATION 21

NUCLEAR REGULATORY COMMISSION 22

DEPARTMENT OF STATE 23

TRANSPORTATION SECURITY ADMINISTRATION 27

PART I – FEDERAL LAWS AND REGULATIONS

EXECUTIVE BRANCH DIRECTIVES REGARDING CLASSIFICATION AND PROTECTION OF FEDERAL INFORMATION

Executive Orders

On April 17, 1995 President William J. Clinton issued Executive Order (EO)12958, which "prescribes a uniform system for classifying, safeguarding, and declassifying national security information." (60 Fed.Reg.19825, April 29, 1995) Section 1.3 establishes classification levels, and Section 1.5 classification categories (types of information eligible for classification). Section 1.8 (b) prohibits the designation of "classified" to be applied to "basic scientific research information not clearly related to the national security." Technical amendments were made by EO 12972 (60 Fed.Reg.48863, September 18, 1995), and EO 13142 (64 Fed.Reg.66089, November 23, 1999).

On March 25, 2003, President George W. Bush issued EO 13292 (68 Fed.Reg.15315, March 28, 2003), amending EO 12958 to "prescribe a uniform system for classifying, safeguarding, and declassifying national security information, including information relating to defense against transnational terrorism." Classification levels (renumbered Section 1.2) remain the same. The list of classification categories (renumbered Section 1.4) redefines "scientific, technological, or economic matters relating to the national security" to include "defense against transnational terrorism," and expands a previous category to now cover "vulnerabilities or capabilities of systems, installations, *infrastructures*, projects, plans, *or protection services* relating to the national security, *which includes defense against transnational terrorism*." (New language in italics.) The text of Section 1.8 (b) is unchanged, but is renumbered Section 1.7 (b).

White House Memoranda

On March 19, 2002, White House Chief of Staff Andrew H. Card, Jr. issued a memorandum to the heads of all executive departments and agencies regarding the safeguarding and protection of sensitive homeland security information. The memo directs recipients to "undertake an immediate reexamination of current measures for identifying and safeguarding" Government information in their respective department or agency "regarding weapons of mass destruction, as well as other information that could be misused to harm the security of our nation and the safety of our people." Agencies are advised that for assistance in applying exemptions of the Freedom of Information Act (FOIA) to sensitive but unclassified information, they should contact the Justice Department's Office of Information and Privacy, or consult OIP's FOIA Web site at http://www.usdoj.gov/04foia/index/html/.

Pursuant to the White House memo, a joint memorandum was issued by the Acting Director of the Information Security Oversight Office and the Co-Directors of the Justice Department's Office of Information and Privacy providing guidance to all departments and agencies as to "safeguarding information regarding weapons of mass destruction and other sensitive records related to homeland security." The memo states that "in addition to information that could reasonably be expected to assist in the development or use of weapons of mass destruction," the classification of which is described elsewhere in the memo, "departments and agencies maintain and control sensitive information related to America's homeland security that might not meet one or more of the standards for classification set forth ... in Executive Order 12958. The need to protect such sensitive information from inappropriate disclosure should be carefully considered, on a case-by-case basis, together with the benefits that result from the open and efficient exchange of scientific, technical, and like information." Agencies are advised to process any FOIA request for records containing "sensitive but unclassified information related to America's homeland security" in accordance with the Attorney General's October 12, 2001 FOIA Memorandum, "by giving full and careful consideration to all applicable FOIA exemptions."

The July 3, 2003 *FOIA Post* (issued by OIP) references a June 25, 2003 FOIA Officers conference at which the above memoranda were described as "placing primary emphasis on the safeguarding of information, where appropriate due to its particular sensitivity rather than on the basis of any catch-all label such as 'sensitive but unclassified information.'"

The above memoranda were posted by the Justice Department on March 21, 2002 at http://www.usdoj.gov/oip/foiapost/2002foiapost10.htm.

Presidential and National Security Directives

Presidential Directive/NSC 24

President Jimmy Carter issued PD/NSC-24 on November 16, 1977, establishing a National Telecommunications Protection Policy. This policy stipulated that "unclassified information transmitted by and between Government agencies and contractors that would be useful to an adversary should be protected." The Secretary of Defense was designated as the Executive Agent for communications security (COMSEC) to "protect government-derived unclassified information, and the Secretary of Commerce as Executive Agent "for communications protection for government-derived unclassified information (excluding that relating to national security)."

This document can be accessed at the Carter Library Web site:
http://www.jimmycarterlibrary.org/documents/pres_directive.phtml

National Security Decision Directive 189 – National Policy on the Transfer of Scientific, Technical and Engineering Information

The Reagan White House issued this directive on September 21, 1985. It states: "It is the policy of this Administration that, to the maximum extent possible, the products of fundamental research remain unrestricted." Fundamental research is defined as basic and applied, non-proprietary or national security research, the results of which are generally published and shared broadly within the scientific community. The directive also states as policy that "where the national security requires control, the mechanism for control of information generated during federally-funded fundamental research in science, technology and engineering at colleges, universities and laboratories is classification."

In a November 1, 2001 letter to the Center for Strategic & International Studies, National Security Advisor Condoleeza Rice stated that until the Bush Administration completes its review of the export control policies that affect basic research, "the policy on the transfer of scientific, technical, and engineering information set forth in NSDD-189 shall remain in effect, and we will ensure that this policy is followed." In an outline of SBU definitions prepared by the Association of American Universities in February 2003, and posted on the Michigan State University Web site, it was reported that Dr. Rice's position was reaffirmed by White House Office of Science and Technology Policy Director Marburger in a talk at the National Academy of Sciences on January 9, 2003.[1] In a May 12, 2003 memorandum to all department heads, Energy Secretary Spencer Abraham recommended the reissuance of NSDD-189, citing Dr. Rice's letter as confirmation that "unless a legal basis exists to control basic research (either by classification or some other means), it shall not be controlled."

National Telecommunications and Information Systems Security Policy (NTISSP) No.2 – National Policy on Protection of Sensitive, but Unclassified Information in Federal Government Telecommunications and Automated Information Systems

This policy directive was issued by National Security Adviser John Poindexter on October 29, 1986, and five months later rescinded by National Security Adviser Frank Carlucci. According to the House Committee considering legislation that later became the Computer Security Act of 1987 (P.L. 100-235), this directive is significant because it "added a new 'sensitive but unclassified' category of Federal information, setting new classification criteria for information formerly unclassified. It would not only have affected managers, users, and programmers of information systems within the Federal Government, but there was concern that it could have been extended to private sector contractors of the Federal Government as well, potentially restricting the type of information and data released."[2]

The text of this directive is contained in Appendix B to *Defending Secrets, Sharing Data: New Locks and Keys for Electronic Information, OTA-CIT-310* (Washington, DC: U.S. Government Printing Office, 1987).

National Security Decision Directive 145 – National Policy on Telecommunications and Automated Information Systems Security

This directive, signed by President Reagan on September 17, 1984, "establishes initial objectives of policies, and an organizational structure to guide the conduct of national activities directed toward safeguarding systems which process or communicate sensitive information from hostile exploitation." In support of the objectives enumerated, a policy is established whereby "systems handling sensitive, but unclassified, government or government-derived information, the loss of which could adversely affect the national security interest, shall be protected in proportion to the threat of exploitation and the associated potential damage to the national security."

---

[1] http://www.msu.edu/unit/vprgs/exportregs.htm

[2] The two House committee reports issued pursuant to H.R. 145 (which became P.L. 100-235) – H.Rept. No. 100-153, part 1 and part 2 – provide extensive background information on the controversy surrounding NTISSP No.2, as well as the testimony the committees received regarding NSDD-145.

The directive establishes a Cabinet-level Systems Steering Group, which will review and evaluate the security status of telecommunications and automated information systems that handle "sensitive government or government-derived information," and "identify categories of sensitive non-government information, the loss of which could adversely affect the national security interest." The Group will also recommend steps to protect this information.

A 1993 GAO report on communications privacy attributes the authorship of this directive to the Department of Defense. In 1985 testimony before Congress, GAO raised concern that the directive "could significantly affect the management of systems by civil agencies and commercial interests" because it failed to define the types of information included in the new SBU category.[3]

NSDD-145 can be accessed at http://www.fas.org/irp/offdocs/nsdd145.htm.

National Security Directive 42 – National Policy for the Security of National Security Telecommunications and Information Systems

This directive was issued by President George H.W. Bush on July 5, 1990. It "establishes initial objectives, policies, and an organizational structure to guide the conduct of activities to secure national security systems from exploitation." It states as policy that "U.S. Government national security systems shall be secured by such means as are necessary to prevent compromise, denial or exploitation."

This directive also rescinds NSDD-145, "except for ongoing telecommunications protection activities mandated by and pursuant to PD-24 and NSDD-145."

NSD-42 can be accessed at http://bushlibrary.tamu.edu/research/nsd/NSD/NSD%2042/0001.pdf.

Future Initiatives

On October 10, 2002, OSTP Director Marburger testified before the House Science Committee on the nexus of homeland security and science.[4] He stated that on the subject of sensitive information, the Office of Homeland Security had asked the Office of Management and Budget "to develop guidance for federal agencies to ensure consistency of treatment of 'sensitive homeland security information' across the Federal Government and by the recipients of such information," e.g., State and local law enforcement personnel. He also testified that the designation Sensitive Homeland Security Information was not a new category of information, but rather "the type of information that the government holds today which is not routinely released to the general public. The vast majority of government information is and will remain publicly accessible." SHSI, because it is not classified information, would have a designation "implemented under existing law and policy, and complements and does not supersede existing mechanisms for classification and de-classification of government information."

---

[3] U.S. General Accounting Office. *Communications Privacy: Federal Policy and Actions*, GAO/OSI-94-2, November 1993.
[4] *Conducting Research During the War on Terrorism: Balancing Openness and Security: Hearing Before the House Comm. On Science*, 107th Cong. 26-27 (2002).

Director Marburger indicated that the Administration had begun meeting with various public interest groups, representatives of State and local government, and the academic community, to garner advice on developing a definition of SHSI. A "guidance document" will be developed by the Administration, and published in the *Federal Register* for comment.

FEDERAL LAWS APPLICABLE TO ALL GOVERNMENT AGENCIES REGARDING SENSITIVE BUT UNCLASSIFIED INFORMATION

Freedom of Information Act of 1966, as Amended (5 USC 552)

Attorney General FOIA Memorandum

On October 12, 2001, Attorney General Ashcroft issued a memorandum to the heads of all federal departments and agencies, providing a new statement of Administration policy on the Freedom of Information Act. It confirms the Administration's commitment to protecting fundamental values –" safeguarding our national security, enhancing the effectiveness of our law enforcement agencies, protecting sensitive business information, and preserving personal privacy." Agencies are encouraged to "carefully consider the protection" of the values and interests enumerated in this memorandum "when making disclosure determinations under the FOIA." Decisions to disclose information protected under the FOIA should be made in consultation with the Department of Justice's Office of Information and Privacy. If any agency decides to withhold records, in whole or in part, Justice will defend this decision "unless it lacks a sound legal basis or presents an unwarranted risk of adverse impact on the ability of other agencies to protect other important records."

This memorandum, and other explanatory material, can be accessed at the Justice Department Office of Information and Privacy *FOIA Post* Web site:
http://www.usdoj.gov/oip/foiapost/2001foiapost19.htm

Exemptions to FOIA

The *Freedom of Information Act Guide, May 2004,* published by the Department of Justice, states that the "Freedom of Information Act generally provides that any person has a right, enforceable in court, to obtain access to federal agency records, except to the extent that such records (or portions of them) are protected from public disclosure by one of nine exemptions or by one of three special law enforcement record exclusions."[5]

Exemption 1 is information classified in the interest of national defense or foreign policy. In the *FOIA Guide* discussion of Exemption 1, federal departments and agencies are advised that in light of the greater emphasis (post-9/11) "placed on the protection of information that could expose the nation's critical infrastructure, military, government, and citizenry to an increased risk of attack," they should "carefully consider the sensitivity of any information the disclosure of which could reasonably be expected to cause national security harm." This guide also notes that categories of homeland-security information like SBU and SHSI have not been classified

---

[5] http://www.usdoj.gov/oip/foi-act.htm

pursuant to EO 12958, and that these terms "might not even fall within any of the FOIA exemptions."

Exemption 2 of the FOIA exempts from mandatory disclosure records that are "related solely to the internal personnel rules and practices of an agency." In the *FOIA Guide* discussion of Exemption 2, it is noted that the courts have interpreted this exemption to include "more substantial internal matters, the disclosure of which would risk circumvention of a legal requirement," and that this category of information "is of fundamental importance to homeland security." The guide enumerates types of information that may warrant Exemption 2 protection, and states that since September 11, the courts have deemed "nonclassified but nonetheless highly sensitive information" exempt from disclosure "in order to avoid the harms described in" Homeland Security Presidential Directive/HSPD-7[6] and the Attorney General's FOIA Memorandum. Contrary to the caveats contained in the discussion of Exemption 1, this section of the guide advises agencies that employ safeguarding labels (like SHSI) for information that has special sensitivity to "carefully consider the propriety of protecting such information under Exemption 2."

Federal Information Security Management Act of 2002 (FISMA)(Public Law 107-347, Title III, 116 Stat. 2899, 2946)

Purpose (Section 301): As stated in the House Committee on Government Reform report accompanying the initial bill, the purpose of this law is "to further strengthen Federal information security by requiring compliance with minimum mandatory management controls for securing information and information systems, clarifying and strengthening current management and reporting requirements, and strengthening the role of the National Institute of Standards and Technology (NIST)." The law also consolidates existing statutory information security requirements, including those contained in the Computer Security Act of 1987.[7]

Definition of information security (Section 301): "Protecting information and information systems from unauthorized access, use, disclosure, disruption, modification, or destruction in order to provide – (A) integrity, which means guarding against improper information modification or destruction, and includes ensuring information nonrepudiation and authenticity; (B) confidentiality, which means preserving authorized restrictions on access and disclosure, including means for protecting personal privacy and proprietary information; and (C) availability, which means ensuring timely and reliable access to an use of information."

Development of Standards and Guidelines (Section 303; 15 U.S.C. 278g-3[8]): NIST is tasked to develop "standards, guidelines, and associated methods and techniques for information systems;

---

[6] 39 Weekly Comp. Pres. Doc. 1816 (December 22, 2003).
[7] H.Rep.No. 107-787, Part 1, at 54 (2002).
[8] Under the provisions of the Computer Security Act of 1987, P.L. 100-235, NIST was given responsibility for developing standards and guidelines for "the protection of sensitive information in Federal computer systems." Although the definition of "sensitive information" contained in that law is often cited as being applicable to SBU information, NIST's mandate has been re-written by the provisions of P.L. 107-347, making this definition moot. Note also that the Bulletin issued by NIST in November 1992 clarifying the meaning of "sensitivity as applied to agency information systems" states that "protecting sensitive information means providing for one or more of the

standards and guidelines, including minimum requirements, for information systems used or operated by an agency (or its contractors); and standards and guidelines, including minimum requirements, for providing adequate information security for all agency operations and assets." These standards and guidelines are to include, "at a minimum:

(1)(A) standards to be used by all agencies to categorize all information and information systems collected or maintained by or on behalf of each agency based on the objectives of providing appropriate levels of information security according to a range of risk levels;

(B) guidelines recommending the types of information and information systems to be included in each such category; and

(C) minimum information security requirements for information and information systems in each such category; and

(2) a definition of and guidelines concerning detection and handling of information security incidents."

Implementation

Pursuant to P.L. 107-347, NIST views its first task as the development of standards to be used by all Federal agencies for categorizing information and information systems. In December 2003, NIST published Federal Information Processing Standards (FIPS) Publication 199, *Standards for Security Categorization of Federal Information and Information Systems* (http://www.csrc.nist.gov/publications/fips/index.html). In this publication, "The security categories are based on the potential impact on an organization should certain events occur which jeopardize the information and information systems needed by the organization to accomplish its assigned mission, protect its assets, fulfill its legal responsibilities, maintain its day-to-day functions, and protect individuals. Security categories are to be used in conjunction with vulnerability and threat information in assessing risk." The publication defines three levels of potential impact—low, moderate, and high—on organizations should there be a breach of security (loss of confidentiality, integrity, or availability).[9]

In December 2003, NIST also issued an initial public draft of Special Publication 800-60, *Guide for Mapping Types of Information and Information Systems,* to assist Federal agencies in identifying information types and information systems, and assigning impact levels for confidentiality, integrity, and availability. Impact levels are based on the security categorization definitions in FIPS Publication 199.[10]

On October 31, 2003, NIST issued an initial draft of Special Publication 800-53, *Recommended Security Controls for Federal Information Systems,* which establishes a set of minimum security controls for low, moderate, and high impact information systems (based on the security

---

following: confidentiality, integrity, and availability." (http://csrc.nist.gov/publications/nistbul/cs192-11.txt) These are the same criteria used in the definition of information security in P.L. 107-347.
[9] NIST Computer Security Division, *2003 Annual Report* (June 2004), http://www.csrc.nist.gov/publications/nistir/IR7111-CSDAnnualReport.pdf. See also *The New FISMA Standards and Guidelines,* written by NIST's Computer Security Division and posted at http://csrc.nist.gov/sec-cert.
[10] http://www.csrc.nist.gov/sec-cert/ca-categorization.html.

categorization definitions in FIPS Publication 199). When completed, this publication will stand as NIST interim guidance until 2005, which is the statutory deadline to publish mandatory minimum security requirements for Federal information systems.[11]

Federal agencies are required under FISMA to use the NIST guidelines (FIPS Publication 199) to define security categories for their information systems. The recommendations for baseline (minimum) security controls published in Special Publication 800-53 "can subsequently be used as a starting point for and input to the organization's risk assessment processes and the development of security plans for those information systems."[12]

Homeland Security Act of 2002 (Public Law 107-296, 116 Stat. 2135)

Statement of Intent: Section 306 (a) stipulates that "to the greatest extent practicable, research conducted or supported by the Department of Homeland Security (DHS) shall be unclassified." President Bush's signing statement accompanying this law states that the executive branch will "construe and carry out" this section, and other provisions of the law, including those addressing information analysis and infrastructure protection, "in a manner consistent with the President's constitutional and statutory authorities to control access to and protect classified information, intelligence sources and methods, sensitive law enforcement information, and information the disclosure of which could otherwise harm the foreign relations or national security of the United States."[13]

TITLE VIII, SUBTITLE I – THE "HOMELAND SECURITY INFORMATION SHARING ACT"

Initial finding: "The Federal Government collects, creates, manages, and protects classified and sensitive but unclassified information to enhance homeland security."

Sharing and identification of information: Section 892 (a) mandates the President to prescribe and implement procedures under which relevant Federal agencies "share relevant and appropriate homeland security information with other Federal agencies, including the Department of Homeland Security, and appropriate State and local personnel, and identify and safeguard homeland security information that is sensitive but unclassified." The President is mandated to ensure that these procedures apply to all agencies of the Federal Government. Section 892 (c)(2) provides that these procedures may include, "with respect to information that is sensitive but unclassified, entering into nondisclosure agreements with appropriate State and local personnel." Authority to promulgate these procedural regulations was delegated to the Secretary of Homeland Security in Executive Order 13311 (July 2003).[14]

---

[11] http://www.csrc.nist.gov/publications/drafts.html.
[12] CSD *2003 Annual Report*, 12.
[13] http://www.whitehouse.gov/news/releases/2002/11/print/20021125-10.html.
[14] 68 Fed.Reg. 45149 (July 31, 2003).

Definition of homeland security information: "Any information possessed by a Federal, State, or local agency that

- (A) relates to the threat of terrorist activity;
- (B) relates to the ability to prevent, interdict, or disrupt terrorist activity;
- (C) would improve the identification or investigation of a suspected terrorist or terrorist organization; or
- (D) would improve the response to a terrorist act."

Report to Congress: Section 893 mandates the President to report to Congress within 12 months on the implementation of Section 892. Pursuant to Executive Order 13311, this function has been delegated to the Secretary of Homeland Security.[15]

Implementing regulations: In a February 18, 2004 letter to the Federation of American Scientists responding to a FOIA request, the Department of Homeland Security stated that pursuant to Section 892 of the Homeland Security Act, the Department was "currently working to develop procedures for the sharing of sensitive homeland security information. However, these procedures have not been finalized."

TITLE II, SUBTITLE B – "CRITICAL INFRASTRUCTURE INFORMATION ACT OF 2002"

Protection of Voluntarily Shared Critical Infrastructure Information: Section 214 provides that "critical infrastructure information (including the identity of a submitting person or entity) that is voluntarily submitted to a covered Federal agency for use by that agency regarding the security of critical infrastructure and protected systems, analysis, warning, interdependency study, recovery, reconstitution, or other informational purpose," shall be exempt from disclosure to the general public under the Freedom of information Act.[16] The term "covered federal agency" refers to the Department of Homeland Security. Critical infrastructure information (CII) is defined to include information "not customarily in the public domain and related to the security of critical infrastructure or protected systems," the interference or incapacitation of which would have a debilitating effect on interstate commerce, national security, or public health or safety. (Section 212).

Implementing Regulations: On February 20, 2004 the Department of Homeland Security issued an interim rule, effective on that date, with request for comments by May 20, 2004, establishing procedures to implement Section 214 of P.L. 107-296 "regarding the receipt, care, and storage of critical infrastructure information voluntarily submitted to the Department of Homeland Security."[17]

---

[15] *FOIA Post* (posted February 27, 2004) reported that this report was submitted to Congress on February 20, 2004. Inquiries to the Department of Homeland Security by this author, to identify and obtain the text of this report, did not receive a response.

[16] See *FOIA Post, Homeland Security Law Contains New Exemption 3 Statute*, posted January 27, 2003, for further discussion of this new exemption to FOIA (http://www.usdoj.gov/oip/foiapost/2003foiapost4.htm).

[17] 69 Fed.Reg.8074 (February 20, 2004).

The proposed rule that the Department had issued on April 15, 2003 (68 Fed.Reg.18523) would have enabled other Federal government entities to act as conduits of CII to DHS. In response to critical comment, the final rule does not allow for indirect submissions. As stated in the introduction to the final rule: "Recognizing that, at this time, implementation of such a provision would present not only operational but, more importantly, also significant program oversight challenges, the Department has removed references throughout the rule to indirect submissions." Revisions have been made to clarify that only DHS and no other Federal government entity shall be the recipient of voluntarily submitted CII. There is, however, a caveat in the introduction that leaves the door open for expanding coverage to other Federal agencies: "After the Protected CII Program has become operational, however, and pending additional legal and related analyses, the Department anticipates the development of appropriate mechanisms to allow for indirect submissions in the final rule and would welcome comments on appropriate procedures for the implementation of indirect submissions."[18] On February 18, 2004 DHS issued a press release announcing the "launch of the Protected Critical Infrastructure Information (PCII) Program."

Internal Directive: Under authority of P.L. 107-296, on May 11, 2004 the Department of Homeland Security issued Management Directive No. 11042. "This directive establishes DHS policy regarding the identification and safeguarding of sensitive but unclassified information originating within DHS. It also applies to other sensitive but unclassified information received by DHS from other government and non-governmental activities."

Although this is an internal directive, it is significant in that it imposes new access controls on Sensitive But Unclassified information, defined as "unclassified information of a sensitive nature, not otherwise categorized by statute or regulation, the unauthorized disclosure of which could adversely impact a person's privacy or welfare, the conduct of Federal programs, or other programs or operations essential to the national interest." This SBU information is identified using the term For Official Use Only (FOUO). The directive enumerates 11 types of information that will be treated as FOUO information, access to which is based on "need-to-know" as determined by the holder of the information. DHS employees, contractors, consultants, and others to whom access is granted will be required to execute a DHS Form 11000-6, Sensitive But Unclassified Information Non-Disclosure Agreement (NdA) upon initial assignment to DHS. Any compromise or unauthorized disclosure of FOUO information will be reported, and inquiries conducted to determine appropriate administrative or disciplinary action.

The text of this directive can be accessed at http://www.fas.org/sgp/othergov/dhs-sbu.html.

EXPORT CONTROLS

Arms Export Control Act/International Traffic in Arms Regulations (ITAR)

The Arms Export Control Act (22U.S.C. 2778 and 2794 (7)) provides authority to designate, and control the export of, defense articles and services. The International Traffic in Arms Regulations (22 CFR Parts 120-130), issued by the State Department pursuant to this law, control the licensing of exports of defense articles, including classified and unclassified technical

---

[18] See also *FOIA Post, Critical Infrastructure Information Regulations Issued by DHS*, posted February 27, 2004, for additional discussion (http://www.usdoj.gov/oip/foiapost/2004foiapost6.htm).

data. All items designated defense articles and defense services constitute the United States Munitions List (USML) (22 CFR Part 121).

Defense article/Technical data defined (22 CFR Part 120.6, Part 126.10, and Part 126.11): A defense article is any item or technical data designated in the Munitions List. Technical data includes "information … required for the design, development, production, manufacture, assembly, operation, repair, testing, maintenance or modification of defense articles." Technical information does not include information in the public domain (defined to include information generally available or accessible to the public through fundamental research).

Defense Service defined (22 CFR Part 120.9): "Furnishing of assistance to foreign persons, in the U.S. or abroad, in the design, development, engineering, manufacture, production, assembly, testing, repair, maintenance, modification, operation, demilitarization, destruction, processing or use of defense articles." Also includes furnishing technical data to foreign nationals.

Licenses for the Export of Defense Articles (22 CFR Part 123)

The transfer of registration or control to a foreign person of any aircraft, vessel, or satellite on the U.S. Munitions List qualifies as an export, and requires a license or written approval from the Office of Defense Trade Controls.

Numerous exemptions are listed that apply to exports of unclassified defense articles for which no approval is needed from the Office of Defense Trade Controls. The exemption for fundamental research was amended in March 2002 pursuant to concerns raised over the March 1999 transfer of licensing jurisdiction for commercial communications satellites to the State Department, placing these satellites on the U.S. Munitions List. This transfer had been mandated by the National Defense Authorization Act Fiscal Year 1999, P.L. 105-121 (Section 1513). The State Department's interim final rule[19] clarified that the transfer to the USML did not change the Department's policy, consistent with NSDD-189, of not regulating fundamental research. Under the ITAR exemption, U.S. accredited institutions of higher learning are permitted to export defense articles fabricated only for fundamental research purposes to similar institutions or government research centers in NATO and major non-NATO ally countries, as long as all the information about the article, including its design, is in the public domain. "For the provision of technical data and defense services, the exemption allows these same institutions the authority to provide defense services related to the assembly and integration of [defense articles fabricated for fundamental research purposes] into a scientific, research or experimental satellite when working with the same set of countries." Prohibited from this exemption are defense services or technical data "for the integration of the satellite or spacecraft to the launch vehicle, or of the Missile Technology Control Regime (MTCR) controlled defense services or technical data."

Sanctions (22CFR Part 127)

Any person convicted of willful violations of export licensing requirements, or making untrue statements of a material fact in license applications, registrations, or reports, shall be subject to a fine or imprisonment, or both.

---

[19] 67 Fed.Reg. 15099 (March 29, 2002).

Export Administration Act/Export Administration Regulations (EAR)

The Export Administration Act of 1979, as amended (50U.S.C.app.2401-2420) provides the statutory authority for the Export Administration Regulations (EAR) administered by the Department of Commerce (15 CFR Parts 730-774). Because the Export Administration Act has expired, and has not yet been reauthorized by Congress, the export licensing system of the Export Administration Act currently operates under authority of the International Emergency Economic Powers Act.[20] The Commerce Department's Bureau of Industry and Security maintains the Commerce Control List (CCL) within the EAR, which includes items (i.e., commodities, software, and technology) controlled for national security purposes, foreign policy controls and short-supply purposes. Items on the CCL cannot be exported to foreign countries without appropriate export license. The CCL is contained in 22 CFR Part 774.

Definition of export of technology or software (15 CFR Part 734.2(b)(2): "Any release of technology or software subject to the EAR in a foreign country, or any release of technology or source code subject to the EAR to a foreign national. An export of technology or source code is 'deemed' to take place when it is released to a foreign national within the United States. Technology or software is 'released' for export when it is available to foreign nationals for visual inspection; when technology is exchanged orally; or when technology is made available by practice or application under the guidance of persons with knowledge of the technology."[21]

Exemption for fundamental research (15 CFR Part 734.8): As in the ITAR, the EAR exempts fundamental research from licensing requirements. "Fundamental research" is defined as "basic and applied research in science and engineering where the resulting information is ordinarily published and shared broadly within the scientific community. It is distinguished from proprietary research and from industrial development, design, production, and product utilization."

Sanctions (15 CFR Part 764.2): Violations of the EAR (e.g., possession of controlled item with intent to export or reexport, evasion or violation of licensing requirements) are subject to civil penalties or denial of export privileges. Willful violations of the EAR's licensing requirements or controls are subject to criminal penalties.

NUCLEAR NONPROLIFERATION

Nuclear Nonproliferation Act (P.L. 95-242)

According to the Commerce Department Bureau of Industry and Security's 2004 Foreign Policy Controls report, the U.S. Government maintains controls on exports of nuclear-related items under the authority of the Nuclear Nonproliferation Act of 1978 (P.L. 95-242) in order to further

---

[20] Executive Order 13222, issued August 17, 2001 (66 Fed.Reg. 44025, August 22, 2001). Presidential Notice of August 6, 2004 (69 Fed.Reg. 48763, August 10, 2004) extends the authorities granted in E0 13222 until August 17, 2005.

[21] The Commerce Department's Bureau of Industry and Security provides answers to frequently asked questions about "deemed exports" at http://www.bxa.doc.gov/DeemedExports/DeemedExportsFAQs.html.

the country's nuclear nonproliferation policy.[22] One of the purposes of P.L. 95-242 is ensuring effective controls by the U.S. over its exports of nuclear materials and equipment and of nuclear technology. The law defines "sensitive nuclear technology" as: "Any information (including information incorporated in a production or utilization facility or important component part thereof) which is not available to the public and which is important to the design, construction, fabrication, operation or maintenance of a uranium enrichment or nuclear fuel reprocessing facility or a facility for the production of heavy water." The law further provides that the export of source material, special nuclear material, production or utilization facilities, and any sensitive nuclear technology, may not be used for any nuclear explosive device or for research on or development of any nuclear explosive device.

Pursuant to this law, the Department of Commerce has adopted licensing requirements: 15 CFR Part 742.3 (CCL Based Controls – Nuclear Nonproliferation) and 15 CFR Part 744.2 (Restrictions on certain nuclear end-uses). These regulations apply to the export of commodities, related technology, or software that either could be of significance for nuclear explosive purposes, or that the exporter knows will be used for nuclear explosive activities or safeguarded or unsafeguarded nuclear activities.

Nuclear Proliferation Prevention Act (P.L. 103-236, Title VIII)

This law imposes sanctions on U.S. and foreign persons who "materially and with requisite knowledge contribute, through the export from the U.S. or any other country of any goods or technology, to the efforts of any individual, group, or non-nuclear-weapon state to acquire unsafeguarded special nuclear material or to use, develop, produce, stockpile, or otherwise acquire any nuclear device." The term "goods and technology" is defined to include "sensitive nuclear technology" as it is defined in P.L. 95-242.

Iran Nonproliferation Act of 2000 (P.L. 106-278)

This law requires the President to report to Congress any foreign person who, on or after January 1, 1999, transfers to Iran either goods, services, or technology listed on control lists of international consortia, e.g., the Missile Technology Control Regime, the Nuclear Suppliers Group, and the Wassenaar Arrangement, or non-controlled goods, services, or technology prohibited for export to Iran because of their "potential to make a material contribution to the development of nuclear, biological, or chemical weapons, or of ballistic or cruise missile systems." Such persons will be prohibited from purchasing any item on the U.S. Munitions List, as well as defense articles and services under the Arms Export Control Act, and will be denied licenses for items controlled by the Export Administration Act Regulations.

MISSILE TECHNOLOGY

Missile Technology Control Regime

According to the Department of Commerce Bureau of Industry and Security (BIS), the Missile Technology Control Regime (MTCR) was created by the United States and six other nations in

---

[22] http://www.bxa.doc.gov/PoliciesAndRegulations/04ForPolControls/Chap12_Nucs.htm

1987 to limit the proliferation of missiles capable of delivering nuclear weapons.[23] It now has 33 member countries. In January 1993, the focus of the Regime was expanded to include missiles for the delivery of chemical or biological weapons, and nuclear weapons. The BIS 2004 Foreign Policy Controls report states that "the MTCR Guidelines and the Equipment, Software and Technology Annex form the basis for U.S. Missile technology controls. The MTCR Guidelines provide licensing policy, procedures, review factors, and standard assurances on missile technology exports. The Annex is a list of missile-related items." A fact sheet prepared by the Department of State Bureau of Nonproliferation indicates that the guidelines "restrict transfers of 'missiles' – defined as rocket systems (including ballistic missiles, space launch vehicles, and sounding rockets) and unmanned aerial vehicle systems capable of delivering weapons of mass destruction – and their related equipment and technology.[24] The full text of both the Guidelines and the Annex can be accessed on the MTCR Web site: http://www.mtcr.info/english/index.html.

The U.S. Government requires a license for the export or reexport to all destinations (except Canada) of those dual-use, i.e., for civilian and military purposes, items specifically identified on the CCL as controlled for missile technology reasons. The relevant sections of the CFR implementing these controls are 15 CFR Part 742.5 (CCL Based controls – Missile Technology) and 15 CFR Part 744.3 (Restrictions on certain missile end-uses). The Export Administration Regulations (EAR) are revised periodically to reflect changes to the MCTR Annex agreed to by member countries at annual plenary sessions. The most recent final rule amends the Commerce Control List (69 Fed.Reg. 24508, May 4, 2004).

National Defense Authorization Act for FY 1991 (P.L. 101-510, Title XVII – Missile Technology Controls)

Public Law 101-510 amends both the Arms Export Control Act and the Export Administration Act to include on the control lists of the ITAR, and EAR, respectively, and require validated licensing for, " all dual use goods and technology on the MTCR Annex, and goods and technology that would provide a direct and immediate impact on the development of missile delivery systems and are not included in the MTCR Annex but which the United States is proposing to the other MTCR adherents to have included in the MTCR Annex." Any foreign or United States person who knowingly violates the abovementioned two acts will be denied licenses for the transfer of missile equipment or technology.

National Defense Authorization Act for FY 1999 (P.L. 105-261, Title XV, Subtitle B – Satellite Export Controls)

This law sets as policy that the United States should not export to the People's Republic of China missile equipment or technology that would improve its space launch capabilities, and requires prior certification of these exports to that effect. It also requires that when licenses are approved for the export of a satellite or related items for launch in a foreign country, the Secretary of Defense must monitor all aspects of the launch to ensure that no unauthorized transfer of technology occurs, including technical assistance and technical data.

---

[23] http://www.bxa.doc.gov/PoliciesandRegulations/04ForPolControls/Chap8_MTCR.htm
[24] http://www.state.gov/t/np/rls/fs/27514.htm

PART II – AGENCY REGULATIONS

DEPARTMENT OF DEFENSE

Unclassifed Information – General

Topic: Definition, Handling, Marking
Document Number: DOD 5200.1-R, AP3 Appendix 3
Document Title: DOD 5200.1-R, Information Security Program, January 1997, Special Types of Unclassified Information Requiring Protection
Source Organization: Department of Defense
Description/Summary: In addition to FOUO and "Sensitive" information, there are other types of information that require application of controls and protective measures for a variety of reasons. This Appendix identifies SBU information from the Department of State, the Drug Enforcement Agency, and DoD Unclassified Controlled Nuclear Information, and explains the nature of the information and the procedures for identifying and controlling it.

When SBU information is included in DoD documents, the documents shall be marked as if the information were For Official Use Only. There is no requirement to remark existing material containing SBU information. Within the Department of Defense, the criteria for allowing access to SBU information are the same as those used for FOUO information.

DEA Sensitive information is unclassified information that is originated by DEA and requires protection against unauthorized disclosure to protect sources and methods of investigative activity, evidence, and the integrity of pretrial investigative reports. The Administrator and certain other officials of the DEA have been authorized to designate information as DEA Sensitive; the Department of Defense has agreed to implement protective measures for DEA Sensitive information in its possession. DEA Sensitive material may be transmitted within CONUS by first class mail. Transmission outside CONUS must be by a means approved for transmission of Secret material. Non-government package delivery and courier services may not be used. The material shall be enclosed in two opaque envelopes or containers, the inner one marked "DEA Sensitive" on both sides. Electronic transmission of DEA Sensitive information within CONUS should be over secure communications circuits whenever possible; transmission outside CONUS must be via approved secure communications circuits.

DoD Unclassified Controlled Nuclear Information (DoD UCNI) is unclassified information on security measures (including security plans, procedures, and equipment) for the physical protection of DoD Special Nuclear Material (SNM), equipment, or facilities. Information is designated DoD UCNI only when it is determined that its unauthorized disclosure could reasonably be expected to have a significant adverse effect on the health and safety of the public or the common defense and security by increasing significantly the likelihood of the illegal production of nuclear weapons or the theft, diversion, or sabotage of DoD SNM, equipment, or facilities.

Access to DoD UCNI shall be granted only to persons who have a valid need-to-know the information and are specifically eligible for access under the provisions of DoD Directive 5210.83. DoD UCNI may be transmitted by first class mail in a single, opaque envelope or

wrapping. Except in emergencies, electronic transmission of DoD UCNI shall be over approved secure communications circuits. Record copies of DoD UCNI documents shall be disposed of in accordance with the Federal Records Act (44 U.S.C. 33) and Component records management directives. Non-record DoD UCNI document may be destroyed by shredding or tearing into pieces and discarding the pieces in regular trash containers. DoD UCNI may be stored in unlocked containers, desks, or cabinets if Government or Government-contract building security is provided, or in locked buildings, rooms, desks, file cabinets, bookcases, or similar items. See also Section on Unclassified Controlled Nuclear Information for U.S. Code and CFR authorities.
Document Source: United States, Department of Defense, "Special Types of Unclassified Information Requiring Protection, AP3 Appendix 3."
Link to Document: www.dod.mil/nii/other/5200_ap3.doc

Topic: Definition, Handling, Procedures
Document Number: DOD 5200.1-R, Appendix C
Document Title: DOD 5200.1-R, Information Security Program, January 1997, Appendix C, Controlled Unclassified Information, Section 1.
Source Organization: Department of Defense
Description/Summary: The requirements of the Information Security Program apply only to information that requires protection to prevent damage to the national security and has been classified in accordance with E.O. 12958 or its predecessors. There are other types of information that require application of controls and protective measures for a variety of reasons. This information is known as "unclassified controlled information." Since classified information and unclassified controlled information exist side-by-side in the work environments – often in the same documents – this appendix is provided as an attempt to avoid confusion and promote proper handling. It covers several types of unclassified controlled information, and provides basic information about the nature of this information and the procedures for identifying and controlling it. In some cases, the appendix refers to other Department of Defense (DoD) Directives that provide more detailed guidance.

The types of information covered in this appendix include "For Official Use Only" information, "Sensitive But Unclassified" (formerly "Limited Official Use") information, "DEA Sensitive Information," "DoD Unclassified Controlled Nuclear Information," "Sensitive Information" as defined in the Computer Security Act of 1987, and information contained in technical documents.
Document Source: Federation of American Scientists, DOD 5200.1-R, Information Security Program, January 1997, "Appendix C, Controlled Unclassified Information, Section 1." http://fas.org/irp/doddir/dod/5200-1r/appendix_c.htm
Link to Document: http://fas.org/irp/doddir/dod/5200-1r/appendix_c.htm

Topic: Safeguards, Markings, Dissemination, Transmission
Document Number: DOD 5400.7R
Document Title: DOD Freedom of Information Act Program, September 1998
Source Organization: Department of Defense
Description/Summary: This regulation is reissued under the authority of DoD Directive 5400.7, DoD Freedom of Information Act (FOIA) Program," September 29, 1997. It provides guidance

on the implementation of the Freedom of Information Act, as amended by the "Electronic Freedom of Information Act Amendments of 1996."

This document describes safeguards to protect sensitive information, which may include SBU information, DoD exemptions to FOIA, specific markings that should be given to sensitive information, and how sensitive information should be disseminated and transmitted.

Document Source: Defense Technical Information Center, DoD 5400.7R, DOD Freedom of Information Act Program, September 1998.
http://www.dtic.mil/whs/directives/corres/pdf/54007r_0998/p54007r.pdf
Link to Document: http://www.dtic.mil/whs/directives/corres/pdf/54007r_0998/p54007r.pdf

Topic: Exemptions
Document Number: 03-CORR-017. March 25, 2003.
Document Title: Memorandum: Subject: Freedom of Information Act (FOIA) Requests for Critical Infrastructure Information (CII).
Source Organization: Department of Defense
Description/Summary: This memorandum states that Exemption 3 of the Homeland Security Act of 2002 does not apply to the Department of Defense. The memorandum lists exemptions for the release of voluntarily submitted critical infrastructure information under the provisions of the Freedom of Information Act.
Document Source: Federation of American Scientists, Department of Defense, Memorandum: Freedom of Information Act (FOIA) Requests for Critical Infrastructure Information (CII).
http://www.fas.org/sgp/foia/dod032503.pdf
Link to Document: http://www.fas.org/sgp/foia/dod032503.pdf

Technical Data

Topic: Definition
Documents: 10 USC 130 - Authority to Withhold from Public Disclosure Certain Technical Data; 32 CFR Part 250 - Withholding of Unclassified Technical Data from Public Disclosure; DoD Directive 5230.25 - Withholding of Unclassified Technical Data from Public Disclosure
Source Organization: Secretary of Defense
Description/Summary: Technical data is defined as a component of critical technology, or militarily critical technology, that "would make a significant contribution to the military potential of any country or combination of countries and that may prove detrimental to the security of the United States." Technical data can be further described as "technical data with military or space application" such as any blueprints, drawings, plans, instructions, computer software and documentation, or other technical information that can be used or be adapted for use to design, engineer, produce, manufacture, operate, repair, overhaul, or reproduce any military or space equipment.
Link to document: http://www.dtic.mil/whs/directives.

Topic: Criteria for withholding technical data
Documents: 10 USC 130 - Authority to Withhold from Public Disclosure Certain Technical Data; 32 CFR Part 250 - Withholding of Unclassified Technical Data from Public Disclosure; DoD Directive 5230.25 - Withholding of Unclassified Technical Data from Public Disclosure
Source Organization: Secretary of Defense
Description/Summary: Determinations regarding the withholding of technical data will be based on whether the data requires an approval, authorization or license for export under E.O. 12470 or the Arms Export Control Act and whether the technical data would disclose critical technology with military or space application. For the latter element, the Militarily Critical Technologies List should be consulted for guidance.
Note: The Militarily Critical Technologies List (MCTL) is a detailed compendium of information on technologies that the Department of Defense assesses as critical to maintaining U.S. military capabilities. The MCTL can be accessed on the web at www.dtic.mil/mctl.
Link to document: http://www.dtic.mil/whs/directives.

Topic: Authorized Dissemination of Technical Data
Documents: 10 USC 130 - Authority to Withhold from Public Disclosure Certain Technical Data; 32 CFR Part 250 - Withholding of Unclassified Technical Data from Public Disclosure; DoD Directive 5230.25 - Withholding of Unclassified Technical Data from Public Disclosure
Source Organization: Secretary of Defense
Description/Summary: Technical data may be released to qualified U.S. contractors when the data relate to a legitimate business purpose, but if the release of such data for purposes other than direct support of DoD activities could jeopardize an important U.S. technological or operational advantage, the data should be withheld. Qualified U.S. contractors may disseminate technical data they have received without prior permission if the purposes for which the data are needed are consistent with their certification. Data may also be disseminated without permission to certain foreign recipients, and to other currently qualified U.S. contractors if the purpose for dissemination is within the scope of certified legitimate business, to the Departments of State and Commerce for specific purposes, to Congress or any Federal, State, or local governmental agency for regulatory purposes or as required by law or court order. Authority must be sought from the controlling DoD office if a contractor needs to disseminate technical data for any other reason.
Note: Parallel Authority for 10 USC 130 is 32 CFR Part 249, "Presentation of DoD-Related Scientific and Technical Papers at Meetings." Unclassified export-controlled DoD technical data may be presented in DoD-related scientific and technical meetings and papers when the recipients are eligible to receive such data as established by 32 CFR Part 250. The same criteria for releasing unclassified documents containing unclassified export-controlled DoD technical data apply to presentations containing such data.
Link to document: http://www.dtic.mil/whs/directives.

Topic: Sanctions
Document Number: 10 USC 130 - Authority to Withhold from Public Disclosure Certain Technical Data; 32 CFR Part 250 - Withholding of Unclassified Technical Data from Public

Disclosure; DoD Directive 5230.25 - Withholding of Unclassified Technical Data from Public Disclosure
Source Organization: Secretary of Defense
Description/Summary: The penalties for unlawful export of information controlled under ITAR or EAR are imprisonment, fines, or both (22 USC 2778; 50 USC app. 2410). Qualified U.S. contractors who commit unauthorized dissemination of information may lose qualified status and may forfeit eligibility for future contracts with DoD.

Topic: Disclaimers
Document Number: 10 USC 130 - Authority to Withhold from Public Disclosure Certain Technical Data; 32 CFR Part 250 - Withholding of Unclassified Technical Data from Public Disclosure; DoD Directive 5230.25 - Withholding of Unclassified Technical Data from Public Disclosure
Source Organization: Secretary of Defense
Description/Summary: No liability will be assumed for patent infringements or misuse of technical data; for loss, damage, or injury resulting from manufacture or use of any product, article, system, or material involving reliance upon any or all technical data; and the adequacy, accuracy, currency, or completeness of the technical data is not guaranteed.

Unclassified Controlled Nuclear Information

Topic: Definition
Documents: 10 U.S.C. 128 - Physical Protection of Special Nuclear Material: Limitation on Dissemination of Unclassified Information; 32 CFR Part 223
Source Organization: Secretary of Defense
Description/Summary: U.S. Code prohibits the unauthorized dissemination of unclassified information pertaining to security measures, including security plans, procedures, and equipment for the physical protection of special nuclear material. A determination must be made that unauthorized dissemination could reasonably be expected to have a significant adverse effect on the health and safety of the public or the common defense and security by significantly increasing the likelihood of illegal production of nuclear weapons; or theft, diversion, or sabotage of special nuclear materials, equipment, or facilities. Title 32 of the Code of Federal Regulations Part 223 implements the authority under 10 USC 128 for controlling unclassified information.

Topic: Protections/Controls
Documents: 10 USC 128 - Physical Protection of Special Nuclear Material: Limitation on Dissemination of Unclassified Information; 32 CFR Part 223.7
Source Organization: Secretary of Defense
Description/Summary: Unclassified documents containing DoD UCNI must be marked appropriately in accordance with the regulations. DoD UCNI may be disseminated in the Office of Defense and various divisions, NATO, and among DoD contractors, consultants, and grantees

on a need-to-know basis. UCNI must be safeguarded during electronic storage, physical storage, destruction of non-record copies, and retirement.

Topic: Sanctions
Documents: 10 USC 128 - Physical Protection of Special Nuclear Material: Limitation on Dissemination of Unclassified Information; 32 CFR Part 223.7
Source Organization: Secretary of Defense
Description/Summary: Unauthorized disclosure of DoD UCNI justifies investigative and administrative actions.

DEPARTMENT OF ENERGY

Topic: Definition
Document Title: Safeguards and Security Glossary of Terms. December 18, 1995
Source Organization: Department of Energy
Description/Summary: Provides a definition of Sensitive Unclassified Information. The definition is as follows: "Information for which disclosure, loss, misuse, alteration, or destruction could adversely affect national security or governmental interests. National security interests are those unclassified matters that relate to the national defense or foreign relations of the U.S. Government. Governmental interests are those related, but not limited to the wide range of government or government-derived economic, human, financial, industrial, agriculture, technological, and law-enforcement information, as well as the privacy or confidentially of personal or commercial proprietary information provided the U.S. Government by its citizens."
Source: United States, Department of Energy
Link to Document: http://www.directives.doe.gov/pdfs/nnglossary/termss_z.pdf

Topic: Definition, Handling
Document Number: None
Document Title: Directives Management Document for Proposed DOE O 471.X, Identifying Information as "For Official Use Only"
Source Organization: Department of Energy
Description/Summary: Directive to establish a program within DOE to identify and mark sensitive unclassified information that may be exempt from public release under the Freedom of Information Act (FOIA) (to be identified as "For Official Use only").
Source: Federation of American Scientists. http://www.fas.org/sgp/news/doesbu.html
Link to Document: http://www.fas.org/sgp/news/doesbu.html

Topic: Definition of Unclassified Controlled Nuclear Information (UCNI)
Documents: 10 CFR Part 1017 - Identification and Protection of Unclassified Controlled Nuclear Information; 42 U.S.C. 2168 - Dissemination of Unclassified Information
Source Organization: Secretary of Energy

Description/Summary: UCNI is defined as certain unclassified government information prohibited from unauthorized dissemination under section 148 of the Atomic Energy Act. Categories include: information concerning production/facility design-related information; security measures for the protection of facilities and nuclear material contained at these facilities or nuclear material in transit; and certain declassified government information concerning the design, manufacture, or use of nuclear weapons that was previously classified as Restricted Data. A Controlling Official will ensure that the information meets specific criteria before it is protected and controlled as UCNI.

Topic: Protections/Controls
Documents: 10 CFR Part 1017 - Identification and Protection of Unclassified Controlled Nuclear Information (UCNI); DOE O 471.2A- U.S. Department of Energy Information Security Program Directive
Source Organization: Secretary of Energy, Department of Energy
Description/Summary: Documents containing UCNI must be marked conspicuously as "Not for Public Dissemination" prior to transmitting or upon retirement. Access is granted on a need-to-know basis. Regulations pursuant to the physical protection of documents while they are in use or storage, being reproduced, being destroyed, or transmitted, must be adhered to in order to prevent unauthorized dissemination.
Link to Document: http://www.oa.doe.gov/sse/directives/o4712a.pdf
Note: DOE O 471.2A expired 09-26-99 but has been extended to 04-28-05 by DOE N 251.57.

Topic: Sanctions
Documents: 10 CFR Part 1017 - Identification and Protection of Unclassified Controlled Nuclear Information; 42 USC 2168 – Dissemination of Unclassified Information; DOE O 471.2A - U.S. Department of Energy Information Security Program
Source Organization: Secretary of Energy, Department of Energy
Description/Summary: Provides civil and criminal penalties for the illegal dissemination of unclassified controlled nuclear information.

FEDERAL AVIATION ADMINISTRATION

Topic: Handling
Document Number: None
Document Title: None
Source Organization: Federal Aviation Administration
Description/Summary: This document lists telecommunications standards to be used by the Federal Aviation Administration (FAA) in the preparation of specifications and related procurement documents that are used when considering the lease or purchase of telecommunications systems, services, or equipment. This document states that equipment and services that are intended for use in the cryptographic protection of sensitive but unclassified computer data shall use one or more of the modes of operation specified in FIPS PUB 81
http://www.itl.nist.gov/fipspubs/fip81.htm.

Document Source: United States, Federal Aviation Administration
Link to Document: http://nasdocs.faa.gov/nasiHTML/FAAStandards/faa-std-029d/029d-txt.html

Topic: Definition, Procedures, Handling
Document Number: 14 CFR Part 193
Document Title: Protection of Voluntarily Submitted Information
Source: 66 FR 33805, June 25, 2001, unless otherwise noted.
Source Organization: Federal Aviation Administration
Description/Summary: This chapter of 14 CFR describes when and how the FAA protects from disclosure safety and security information that is submitted voluntarily to the FAA. This chapter carries out 49 USC 40123, protection of voluntarily submitted information.
Document Source: United States, Government Printing Office
Link to Document: http://www.access.gpo.gov/nara/cfr/waisidx_04/14cfr193_04.html

NUCLEAR REGULATORY COMMISSION

Topic: Definition, Access
Document Number: COMSECY-02-0015 (April 4, 2002)
Document Title: Commission Action Memorandum: Withholding Sensitive Homeland Security Information From the Public
Source Organization: Nuclear Regulatory Commission
Description/Summary: Provides guidance and criteria to be used when considering the release of potentially sensitive information. The definition of SHSI is based on draft DHS language (not made public). Generally, information generated by the NRC, its licensees, or contractors will be withheld if its release could provide a clear and significant benefit to an adversary in a potential attack, but information of a general nature will not be withheld. More specifically, information that is currently widely available to the public should not be systematically reviewed against the criteria established in this memorandum; documents that were withdrawn from the NRC external web page, the public library of ADAMS, or the public document room in response to 9/11 events, will be reviewed against the criteria prior to re-release; and all newly generated documents will be reviewed against certain criteria. Criteria include: plant-specific information that would clearly aid in planning an assault on a facility; physical vulnerabilities of nuclear facilities; construction details of specific facilities; information that would be useful for breaching key barriers at nuclear facilities; and information in any type of document that provides the current status or configuration of systems and equipment (except general conditions such as 100 percent power or shutdown).
Source: United States, Nuclear Regulatory Commission
Link to Document: http://www.nrc.gov/reading-rm/doc-collections/commission/comm-secy/2002/2002-0015comscy.pdf

Topic: Definition, Access
Document Number: Memorandum, 05-28-2002

Document Title: Commission Action Memorandum, 05-28-2002, Approving COMSECY-02-0015
Source Organization: Nuclear Regulatory Commission
Description/Summary: Memorandum approving criteria proposed in COMSECY-02-0015 - "Withholding Sensitive Homeland Security Information From the Public."
Source: United States, Nuclear Regulatory Commission
Link to Document: http://www.nrc.gov/reading-rm/doc-collections/commission/comm-secy/2002/2002-0015comsrm.pdf

DEPARTMENT OF STATE

Topic: Definition
Document Number: Volume 12 Foreign Affairs Manual 540. TL:DS-46; 05-26-1995
Document Title: Scope
Source Organization: Department of State
Description/Summary: Defines Sensitive But Unclassified information: "SBU describes information which warrants a degree of protection and administrative control that meets the criteria for exemption from public disclosure set forth under Sections 552 and 552a of Title 5, United States Code: the Freedom of Information Act and the Privacy Act.
b. SBU information includes, but is not limited to:
(1) Medical, personnel, financial, investigatory, visa, law enforcement, or other information which, if released, could result in harm or unfair treatment to any individual or group, or could have a negative impact upon foreign policy or relations; and
(2) Information offered under conditions of confidentiality which arises in the course of a deliberative process (or a civil discovery process), including attorney-client privilege or work product, and information arising from the advice and counsel of subordinates to policy makers."
Source: United States Department of State, Volume 12 FAM 540, "Sensitive But Unclassified Information (SBU)," TL:DS-61; 1--01-1999.
Link to Document: http://foia.state.gov/masterdocs/12fam/12m0540.pdf

Topic: Implementation
Document Number: Volume 12 Foreign Affairs Manual 542. TL:DS-46; 05-26-1995
Document Title: Implementation
Source Organization: Department of State
Description/Summary: States that regulations regarding "Limited Official Use" (LOU) are superseded and LOU becomes Sensitive But Unclassified (SBU) as of the date of publication.
Source: United States Department of State, Volume 12 FAM 540, "Sensitive But Unclassified Information (SBU)," TL:DS-61; 1--01-1999.
Link to Document: http://foia.state.gov/masterdocs/12fam/12m0540.pdf

Topic: Controls
Document Number: Volume 12 Foreign Affairs Manual 543. TL:DS-46; 10-01-1999
Document Title: Access, Dissemination, and Release.

Source Organization: Department of State
Description/Summary: U.S. citizen direct-hire supervisory employees are responsible for access, dissemination, and release of SBU material. Employees will limit access to protect SBU information from unintended public disclosure.

Employees may circulate SBU material to others, including Foreign Service nationals, to carry out an official U.S. Government function if not otherwise prohibited by law, regulation, or interagency agreement.

SBU information is not required to be marked, but should carry a distribution restriction to make the recipient aware of specific controls. To protect SBU information stored or processed on automated information systems, the requirements found in 12 FAM 600 (Information Security Technology) must be met.
Source: United States Department of State, Volume 12 FAM 540, "Sensitive But Unclassified Information (SBU)," TL:DS-61; 1--01-1999.
Link to Document: http://foia.state.gov/masterdocs/12fam/12m0540.pdf

Topic: Controls
Document Number: Volume 12 Foreign Affairs Manual 544. TL:DS-46; 06-08-1995
Document Title: Sensitive But Unclassified Handling Procedures: Transmission, Mailing, Safeguarding/Storage, and Destruction
Source Organization: Department of State
Description/Summary: Regardless of method, transmission of SBU information should be effected through means that limit the potential for unauthorized public disclosure. Since information transmitted over unencrypted electronic links such as telephones may be intercepted by unintended recipients, custodians of SBU information should decide whether specific information warrants a higher level of protection accorded by a secure fax, phone, or other encrypted means of communication.

SBU information may be sent via the U.S. Postal Service, APO, commercial messenger, or unclassified registered pouch, provided it is packaged in a way that does not disclose its contents or the fact that it is SBU.

During nonduty hours, SBU information must be secured within a locked office or suite, or secured in a locked container.

SBU documents must be destroyed by shredding or burning, or by other methods consistent with law or regulation.
Source: United States Department of State, Volume 12 FAM 540, "Sensitive But Unclassified Information (SBU)," TL:DS-61; 1--01-1999.
Link to Document: http://foia.state.gov/masterdocs/12fam/12m0540.pdf

Topic: Consequences
Document Number: Volume 12 Foreign Affairs Manual 545. TL:DS-46; 05-26-1995
Document Title: Responsibilities
Source Organization: Department of State
Description/Summary: Provides a general warning of consequences for person or persons guilty of unauthorized disclosure of Sensitive But Unclassified information. Provides references to Foreign Affairs Manuals that provide specific information on regulations, processes and

penalties for person or persons guilty of unauthorized disclosure of Sensitive But Unclassified information.
Source: United States Department of State, Volume 12 FAM 540, "Sensitive But Unclassified Information (SBU)," TL:DS-61; 1--01-1999.
Link to Document: http://foia.state.gov/masterdocs/12fam/12m0540.pdf

Topic: Definition, Handling, and Procedure
Document Number: Executive Order 12958: Telegram Ref: 95 State 232445. 02/02/2000
Document Title: Department of State Telegram, to All Diplomatic and Consular Posts US Office Pristina Special Embassy Program. Guidance For Drafting Sensitive But Unclassified Telegram
Source Organization: Department of State
Description/Summary: Describes how documents containing sensitive but unclassified information should be labeled.
Source: United States, Department of State, "Executive Order 12958: Telegram Ref: 95 State 232445. 02/02/2000." Federation of American Scientists.
http://www.fas.org/sgp/news/2000/02/sbu.html
Link to Document: www.fas.org/sgp/news/2000/02/sbu.html

Topic: Transmission and Handling
Document Number: Volume 5 Foreign Affairs Manual 751.2. TL:IM-39; 06-13-2003
Document Title: Email: Prohibitions When Using Email
Source Organization: Department of State
Description/Summary: Sensitive But Unclassified (SBU) e-mail may be transmitted on the unclassified INTRANET. SBU information marked NOFORN or with other restricted distribution must be transmitted on the classified INTRANET. SBU e-mail may not be transmitted over the INTERNET.
Source: United States Department of State, Volume 5 Foreign Affairs Manual 751.2. TL:IM-39; 06-13-2003, "Email: Prohibitions When Using Email."
http://foia.state.gov/masterdocs/05FAM/05M0750.PDF
Link to Document: http://foia.state.gov/masterdocs/05FAM/05M0750.PDF

Topic: Transmission
Document Number: Volume 12 Foreign Affairs Manual 660. TL:DS-52; 4-19-1996
Document Title: Communications Security (COMSEC) (SBU)
Source Organization: Department of State
Description/Summary: This subchapter has been designated Sensitive But Unclassified—NOFORN, and it is not included in the CD-ROM or available online. Attempts were made to gain a hard copy of this section of the Manual, but the Department of State would not release the information for security reasons.
Source: United States Department of State, Volume 12 Foreign Affairs Manual 660. TL:DS-52; 4-19-1996, "Communications Security (COMSEC) (SBU)."
http://foia.state.gov/masterdocs/12fam/12m0660.pdf

Link to Document: http://foia.state.gov/masterdocs/12fam/12m0660.pdf

Topic: Sanctions
Document Number: Volume 3 Foreign Affairs Manual 4300.
Document Title: Disciplinary Action (Including Separation for Cause)
Source Organization: Department of State
Description/Summary: Section 4300 contains the following subsections that deal with various aspects of disciplinary action: 4310 Disciplinary Action-General; 4320 Disciplinary Action Common Practices; 4330 Admonishment; 4340 Reprimand; 4350 Suspension; 4360 Separation for Cause; 4370 List of Offenses Subject to Disciplinary Action Foreign Services. No one subsection details specific sanctions or procedures for responding to the improper or unauthorized release of SBU; however all section are relevant since they describe the sanctions and procedures for responding to the improper or unauthorized release or handling of information generally.
Source: United States Department of State, Volume 3 FAM, "Disciplinary Action (Including Separation for Cause)." http://foia.state.gov/REGS/fams.asp?level=2&id=3&fam=0
Link to Document: U.S. Department of State FOIA Electronic Reading Room

Topic: Handling, Transmission
Document Number: Volume 12 Foreign Affairs Manual 620. TL:DS-87; 01-08-2003
Document Title: Unclassified Automated Information Systems
Source Organization: Department of State
Description/Summary: Procedures for transmission of SBU over the Unclassified Automated Information System.
Source: United States Department of State, Volume 12 FAM 620, "Unclassified Automated Information Systems."
Link to Document: http://foia.state.gov/masterdocs/12fam/12m0620.pdf

Topic: Marking, Transmission, Handling
Document Number: 5 FAH-1 H-135 *(TL:CH-4; 07-31-2002)*
Document Title: Administrative Control Marking
Source Organization: Department of State
Description/Summary: The administrative control designation (SBU) protects documents that do not contain national security information, but must be protected from disclosure. This control designation must appear at the top and bottom of any cover, title page, first page, and last page of the document. See 12 FAM 540 for further information; see 5 FAH-1 H-200 for SBU telegrams.
Source: United States Department of State, Volume 5 FAH 620, "Administrative Control Marking."
Link to Document: http://www.foia.state.gov/masterdocs/05fah01/CH0130.pdf

Topic: Marking, Handling
Document Number: 5 FAH-1 H-200 and 5 FAH-1 H-210 *(TL:CH-09; 07-12-2004)*

Document Title: Volume 5 Foreign Affairs Handbook 1 H-200, TELEGRAMS and Volume 5 Foreign Affairs Handbook 1 H-210, HOW TO USE TELEGRAMS *(TL:CH-09; 07-12-2004)*
Source Organization: Department of State
Description/Summary: Details how to mark and handle telegrams containing SBU.
Source: United States, Department of State, Volume 5 Foreign Affairs Handbook 1 H-200, "Telegrams" and Volume 5 Foreign Affairs Handbook 1 H-210, "How To Use Telegrams."
Link to Document: http://www.foia.state.gov/masterdocs/05fah01/CH0210.pdf

TRANSPORTATION SECURITY ADMINISTRATION

Topic: Definition – Sensitive Security Information (SSI)
Documents: 49 CFR 1520 – Protection of Sensitive Security Information
Source Organization: Transportation Security Administration
Description/Summary: Sensitive Security Information (SSI) is defined as information obtained or developed during security activities, the disclosure of which would constitute an unwarranted invasion of privacy, reveal trade secrets or privileged or confidential information, or be detrimental to the security of transportation. Such information includes: security programs and contingency plans, security directives, information circulars, performance specifications, vulnerability assessments, security inspection or investigative information, threat information, security measures, security screening information, security training materials, identifying information relating to certain transportation security personnel, critical aviation or maritime infrastructure asset information, systems security information, confidential business information, information obtained from research and development activities, or any information that TSA determines is SSI under 49 U.S.C. 114(s) or that the Secretary of DOT determines is SSI under 49 U.S.C. 40119.
Note: TSA's final rule, 67 Fed. Reg. 8340, February 22, 2002, transfers the FAA's rules governing civil aviation security to TSA and amends the former FAA rules to enhance security as required by the Aviation and Transportation Security Act (ATSA), P.L. 107-71. Because of this transferal, rules for protecting sensitive security information will now be found in 49 CFR 1520, replacing 14 CFR 191. Also of note: an interim final rule was published in the May 18, 2004 Federal Register (69 Fed. Reg. 28066), further revising 49 Fed. Reg. 1520 in order to protect the confidentiality of maritime security measures that were adopted under the U.S. Coast Guard's regulations, which implement the Maritime Transportation Security Act (MTSA). By issuing this interim final rule, TSA is expanding the scope of its SSI regulation to cover security measures required by the MTSA regulations.

Topic: Protection and Control of SSI
Documents: 49 CFR 1520 – Protection of Sensitive Security Information
Source Organization: Transportation Security Administration
Description/Summary: Persons subject to the requirements of part 1520 are considered "covered persons" who have a duty to protect information by adhering to restrictions on the disclosure of SSI. To this end, a covered person must take reasonable steps to safeguard SSI, may disclose or provide access to SSI only to other covered persons with a need to know, must

mark SSI in a specified manner, dispose of SSI in a specified manner, and report unauthorized disclosures.

Topic: Authorized Disclosure
Documents: 49 CFR 1520 – Protection of Sensitive Security Information
Source Organization: Transportation Security Administration
Description/Summary: Records containing SSI are not available for public inspection except when disclosure is specifically authorized. For example, the TSA or Coast Guard may disclose redacted SSI records in response to a proper FOIA or Privacy Act request, in certain enforcement proceedings, and when a conditional disclosure would not be detrimental to transportation security. Disclosures to committees of Congress and the Government Accountability Office are not precluded by this regulation.

Topic: Sanctions
Documents: 49 CFR 1520 – Protection of Sensitive Security Information
Source Organization: Transportation Security Administration
Description/Summary: Consequences of unauthorized disclosure of SSI include civil penalties and other enforcement or corrective action by DHS, and appropriate personnel actions for Federal employees.

www.ingramcontent.com/pod-product-compliance
Lightning Source LLC
Chambersburg PA
CBHW081812170526
45167CB00008B/3412